·TESCO·COOKERY·COLLECT

NEW MICROWA COOKING

MICROWAVE & COMBINATION

TESCO

CONTENTS

NOTE

Standard spoon measurements are used in all recipes

1 tablespoon (tbls) = one 15 ml spoon
1 teaspoon (tsp) = one 5 ml spoon
All spoon measures are level

All eggs are sized 3 or 4 (standard) unless otherwise stated.

For all recipes, quantities are given in both metric and imperial measures. Follow either set but not a mixture of both, as they are not interchangeable.

Following the success of the first 20 books we produced in the Tesco Cookery Collection, we are delighted to be adding 4 new titles to this exciting series. As before, it is the close contact we have with our customers and the feedback we have had through our Consumer Advisory Kitchens which has helped us to select these latest titles. Each one focuses on an area in which our customers have shown particular interest and contains practical background information on the chosen subject together with a wide selection of carefully tested recipes, each one illustrated in colour.

Microwave cookers are here to stay and new developments are arriving on the market all the time. Perhaps the most exciting of these is the combination oven, providing conventional or microwave cooking or a combination of both at the touch of a button. In *New Microwave Cooking*, our follow up to the successful *Microwave Cooking*, we cover this revolutionary and versatile new area of cookery, as well as providing more recipes for cooking by microwave power alone. The recipes are divided into Microwave and Combination sections and have been selected to suit the two different styles of cooking. Wherever possible, combination recipes also have instructions for cooking with a microwave together with a conventional oven. I hope that microwave users, new and old, will enjoy looking through these pages and trying out the recipes. Enjoy your cooking!

Carey Dennis, Head of Product and Consumer Services at Tesco

INTRODUCTION

The microwave oven is probably one of the most versatile cooking appliances available.

It is useful for the single person, for couples and families, providing meals at all times of the day with minimal fuss and within minutes.

Microwave ovens are fast: they can save up to three-quarters of normal cooking times. Combination microwave ovens will save between a third and a half of the normal time, but have the advantage of producing browned and crispy food. Both these ovens are economical, since they reduce the cooking time.

Microwave and combination ovens are invaluable when it comes to menu planning: both have a defrost facility, so foods can be taken straight from the freezer and defrosted in minutes. They are also ideal for reheating food.

An important factor in today's diet is its nutritional value. Microwave cooking requires little additional liquid and very little fat, if any; this advantage, combined with the speed of microwave cooking, keeps the nutrional value high and makes for a healthier diet. Combination cooking browns a number of foods without the addition of extra fat, which is another plus point for this form of cookery.

WHAT ARE MICROWAVES?

Microwave energy is a type of electrical energy, similar to radio waves but shorter, which is why they are called 'micro'-waves. They are set into action only after the oven door has been closed and a programme selected and started. They are produced by converting electrical energy from the household power supply into high frequency microwaves.

HOW DO MICROWAVES WORK?

Microwaves are absorbed by water, fat and sugar molecules in food. This creates rapid friction which produces heat. Microwaves penetrate to a depth of 4-5 cm (1½-2 inches) so foods with a greater depth are cooked in the middle by conduction.

Combination ovens have this microwave cooking feature, but also incorporate conventional cooking. The oven combines the speed of the microwave with cooking by the convection of hot air to brown food.

TYPES OF COMBINATION OF OVEN

The most sophisticated combination ovens combine microwave and convection cooking in the same process. These are known as *simultaneous* combination cookers. These ovens will cook either by microwave alone, convection alone or in simultaneous combination. The end result is food which is indistinguishable from conventionally cooked food, produced in half to two-thirds the time. The recipes from the combination section of this book have been tested in this type of combination oven. (See notes for the user pp. 8-9).

There is another type of combination oven known as a *sequence* combination oven. Here the two methods of cooking may be used separately or in tandem–convection followed by microwave or microwave followed by convection, repeating throughout the cooking process. This type of oven is less versatile and will not produce good results with certain foods (such as soufflés) which rise during cooking.

Some combination ovens also incorporate grill features.

COOKING TECHNIQUES
Foods need to be stirred and turned as in conventional cooking to ensure even heating. Covering foods when using the microwave cooking method helps to speed up the cooking process.

Most foods cooked by microwave energy require standing time. This varies from a few seconds to 15-20 minutes with large joints of meat. Standing time is reduced and in many cases unnecessary with combination cooking.

Timing relates to the quantity, temperature and type of food, particularly with microwave cooking. It is important to check food, for it is impossible to put right food that has been overcooked.

Aluminium foil containers should not be used for microwave cooking but may be used for combination cooking. Again, check the manufacturer's instructions as to where these should be placed in the oven. Some suggest the turntable and others the wire rack. Foil containers are ideal for convection cooking.

You may find that many recipes call for more than one type of cooking process. For instance a dish may be cooked by microwave energy but browned under the grill, so take this into consideration when selecting the type of dish required.

SUITABLE COOKWARE

Choosing the right container is important to ensure good results. The requirements vary, however, according to the cooking method. Many of the containers and materials normally found in the kitchen can be used for one or more of the cooking processses. Bear in mind that the size and material of the container can make a difference to the cooking time.

Glassware

For general use, whether it is microwave, combination or convection, use heat-resistant glassware. Glass dishes have the added bonus of keeping the food visible. Do not, however, use lead crystal or silver-rimmed dishes as metal can cause arcing (see 'Metal cookware').

China, ceramic and earthenware

All ovenproof china, ceramic and earthenware are suitable for use with each cooking method. Remember to avoid the use of dishes with metal decorations when cooking with microwave energy. Unglazed and partially glazed earthenware are unsuitable as the water in the clay attracts the microwave energy.

Plastics and microwave-ware

Ideal for microwave use, but do not use them for foods which reach very high temperatures, e.g. sugar syrups. You can look for the label 'dishwasher safe' as a useful guide to their suitability for microwave use.

The use of microwave-ware and plastics is limited with combination and convection cooking, as most will not withstand the heat. Check the manufacturer's recommendations.

Roasting bags can be used for all three cooking processes. Clear stretch film, however, may be used for microwave cooking only. There are several different kinds of stretch film available. Choose a plasticiser-free stretch film in preference to cling film, or if using cling film make sure that it is not touching the food during cooking. Remember to pierce roasting bags and stretch film to allow steam to escape.

Browning dishes should only be used on the microwave setting.

Paper, cotton, linen, straw

These items all fall into the wide range of cooking utensils that are microwave safe only. Greaseproof paper and absorbent kitchen paper are ideal as loose coverings to minimise splattering when cooking foods like bacon.

Uncoloured paper napkins can be used as a base for heating breads or croissants, as can linen and cotton napkins and straw baskets. Do not subject them to excessive microwave energy. Paper cups and plates are also ideal for reheating; in fact paper cups make useful cookware items for sponge puddings!

Avoid wax-coated paper, as the wax will melt in the heat transferred from the food.

Metal cookware

Metal is unsuitable for microwave cooking. The use of metal cookware for *combination* cooking varies between manufacturers. Opinions differ between never using it, using it to a limited extent and almost unlimited use. It is very important that you follow the manufacturer's instructions or use non-metallic containers if you are unsure.

During combination cooking where metal is allowed, some tins may arc where they come into contact with the turntable or accessory racks. Arcing is a discharge of electricity and should be avoided. To eliminate it, place the tin on top of a heatproof ceramic or glass plate. If arcing still occurs, do not use the tin for combination cooking.

Aluminium foil
Small pieces of smooth aluminium foil may be used to shield vulnerable parts of food such as chicken wing tips and legs and fish heads and tails, to prevent overcooking. It should be used sparingly when the cooking process includes microwave energy, and should not touch any other pieces of metal in the oven.

NOTES FOR THE USER
The microwave recipes in this book have been tested in a 650 watt cooker with High, Medium-High, Medium, Medium-Low and Low settings. (See Wattage).

The combination recipes in this book have been tested in a 650 watt *simultaneous* combination cooker (see page 5) which has **combination** High and Low settings. These

settings equal 30% and 10% microwave energy and used *in combination with* the convection temperature settings ranging from 160°C to 250°C. The full range of convection and microwave settings are available when these functions are used on their own.

Although most of these recipes can also be cooked in a *sequence* combination cooker the timings will be different, so readers with sequence cookers or ordinary microwaves should follow the ***Microwave plus conventional*** and ***Microwave only*** instructions which have been given where applicable. The conventional instruction is for browning in a conventional oven or under the grill after microwaving.

SELECTING THE BEST COOKING METHOD

Not all foods can be cooked perfectly by the same method, so use the best one for each food.

WATTAGE

If you have a cooker with higher or lower wattage the following should be followed *when using the microwave function:*

- For a 500 watt cooker increase the cooking time by 15-20 seconds per minute.
- For a 700 watt cooker decrease the cooking time by about 5 seconds per minute.

Microwave cooking is perfect for foods which do not require a crispy or brown finish. Because the speed of the microwave energy seals in moisture, it retains the flavour of fish and vegetables superbly.

Other foods which are ideal for microwave cooking include soups, sauces, egg dishes, minced meat dishes, rice, pasta and preserves.

Defrosting of frozen foods and reheating of plated meals and some convenience foods are obvious areas for microwave cookery.

The combination cooker comes into its own with foods which require browning. All types of pastries, pies, flans, tarts and puddings, whether home-made or

ready-prepared convenience foods, benefit from the combination method. Roasts, casseroles, cakes, biscuits, breads and breadcrumb toppings also work well.

Frozen pies and convenience foods cook in half to two-thirds the time required by conventional cooking, and in many cases preheating of the oven is unnecessary.

There are a few foods which are still best cooked conventionally. These include deep-fat frying, boiled eggs and meringues.

COMBINATION COOKING TIMES FOR CONVENIENCE FOODS

Food Item	Weight	Setting	Time	Additional Information
Smoked Haddock crumble	400 g/ 14.1 oz	230°C/ 30% m-wave	25 mins	Place on wire rack; stand for 5 mins. before serving.
Fish fingers	283 g/ 10 oz	250°C/ 30% m-wave	12-14 mins	Place on turntable
Cornish pasties, uncooked	4 × 175 g/ 6 oz	230°C/ 30% m-wave	20-25 mins	Brush with milk and place on turntable
Cheese, egg and bacon flan, uncooked	312 g/ 11 oz	220°C/ 30% m-wave	20 mins	Place on wire rack
Family meat pie, uncooked	750 g/ 1½ lb	180°C/ 30% m-wave	25-30 mins	Place on turntable Brush top with milk
Cauliflower cheese	284 g/ 10 oz	220°C/ 30% m-wave	25-30 mins	Place on wire rack
Cannelloni	350 g/ 12 oz	230°C/ 30% m-wave	25 mins	Decand into a similar sized dish to cook
Turkey grillsteaks (2)	210 g/ 7.4 oz	Preheat to 230°C 230°C/ 30% m-wave	12 mins	Place on wire rack
Beefburgers (4)	227 g/ 8 oz	Preheat to 200°C 250°C/ 30% m-wave	6-7 mins	Place on turntable
Shepherds pie	454 g/ 1 lb	250°C/ 30% m-wave	30-35 mins	Place on wire rack
Individual meat pie, uncooked	154 g/ 5½ oz	230°C/ 30% m-wave	15-17 mins	Brush with milk and place on wire rack
Toad in the hole	170 g/ 6 oz	Preheat to 230°C 230°C/ 10% m-wave	20-25 mins	Place on turntable
Oven chips	225 g/ 8 oz	Preheat to 230°C 250°C/ 30% m-wave	8 mins	Place on turntable in a single layer
Oven chips	450 g/ 1 lb		10 mins	
Fruit crumble	400 g/ 14.1 oz	230°C/ 30% m-wave	25 mins	Place on turntable
Fruit pie	438 g/ 15.4 oz	230°C/ 30% m-wave	25 mins	Place on wire rack

Savoury baked eggs

SERVES 4

4 eggs
50 g (2 oz) small button mushrooms, chopped
50 g (2 oz) smoked ham, diced
2 tsp fresh chopped parsley
salt and pepper

Divide the mushrooms, ham and the parsley between 4 individual ramekin dishes. Season and break an egg into each dish.

Prick the egg yolks with a cocktail stick. Three-quarters cover the dishes with stretch film and place around the edge of the turntable.

Microwave on **Medium** for 5-5½ minutes, or until the whites of the eggs are almost set. Leave to stand for 1-2 minutes for the whites to set. Remove the stretch film and serve.

Serving idea: Serve with hot buttered toast.

Variation: Replace the mushrooms with chopped spring onions.

• **Savoury baked eggs**

Cream of pimento soup

SERVES 4

2 large red peppers, seeded and chopped
2 tbls vegetable oil
2 onions, chopped
3 tbls plain flour
750 ml (1¼ pints) hot vegetable stock
3 tbls tomato purée
salt and pepper
4 tbls single cream
To garnish
1 tbls chopped green pepper
1 tbls chopped red pepper

Place the peppers, oil and onions in a large casserole, cover and microwave on **High** for 6 minutes, stirring twice. Stir in the flour. Gradually add the stock, stirring continuously.

Add the tomato purée and microwave on **High** for 4-5 minutes or until thickened, stirring 3 or 4 times. Cover and microwave on **Medium** for 5 minutes.

Allow the soup to cool slightly, then purée in a food processor or electric blender. Rinse out the casserole dish and pour the soup back in. Season to taste and microwave on **High** for 1 minute.

Stir in the cream, adjust the seasoning and serve in individual bowls garnished with chopped peppers.

Serving idea: Serve with warmed crusty rolls.

Variation: Replace the fresh red peppers with the equivalent of 2 canned pimentos. Drain, chop and use as for red peppers.

Mediterranean soup

SERVES 4

225 g (8 oz) cod, skinned and diced
100 g (4 oz) shelled prawns
2 tbls olive oil
2 cloves garlic, crushed
2 onions, sliced
1 small aubergine, chopped
2 tbls tomato purée
397 g (14 oz) can tomatoes
2 celery sticks, sliced
250 ml (8 fl oz) dry white wine
1 tbls chopped flat leaf parsley
1 tsp dried oregano
salt and pepper
25 g (1 oz) Parmesan cheese, grated (optional)
chopped flat leaf parsley, to garnish

Place the oil, garlic and onions in a 2.4 litre (4 pint) casserole dish and microwave on **High** for 4 minutes, stirring twice. Add the aubergine and microwave on **High** for 2 minutes.

Add the tomato purée, tomatoes with their juice, celery, wine, parsley and oregano, and 120 ml (4 fl oz) water. Cover and microwave on **High** for 10 minutes.

Add the cod and prawns and season to taste. Microwave on **High** for 3 minutes.

Stir in the Parmesan cheese if using and serve in individual bowls, garnished with chopped flat leaf parsley.

Variation: Replace the cod with any variety of white fish. Smoked cod or haddock are also suitable. Shrimps can be used instead of prawns. Canned or frozen shellfish can be substituted for fresh prawns.

• **Cream of pimento soup; Chinese style chicken wings; Mediterranean soup**

Chinese style chicken wings

SERVES 4

8 chicken wings
2 tbls clear honey
2 tbls soy sauce
2 tbls dry sherry
1 small clove garlic, crushed
2.5 cm (1 inch) piece root ginger, peeled and grated
2 tsp cornflour
150 ml (5 fl oz) orange juice
3 spring onions, green tops only, cut diagonally
2 mandarin oranges, peeled, pith removed and segmented
salt and cayenne pepper
4 spring onions, to garnish

Mix the honey, soy sauce, sherry, garlic and ginger together. Leave the chicken wings to marinade in this, in a covered dish, for 2 hours.

Place the chicken wings on a roasting rack. Reserve the marinade.

Microwave the chicken on **High** for 6-7 minutes, or until the juices run clear when the thickest part of the wing is pierced with a knife.

Mix the cornflour with 1 tbls orange juice then add the remaining juice. Mix with the reserved marinade and microwave on **High** for 2 minutes, or until thickened, stirring 2-3 times. Stir in half the onions, the mandarin segments and seasoning.

Serve the chicken wings with the sauce poured over them and garnished with the remaining onions.

• **French bean salad; Stuffed mushrooms; Mussels in white wine**

Stuffed mushrooms

SERVES 4

8 large flat mushrooms, wiped
50 g (2 oz) long grain rice
300 ml (½ pint) boiling salted water
25 g (1 oz) butter or margarine
4 spring onions, chopped
75 g (3 oz) frozen sweetcorn, defrosted
75 g (3 oz) Lymeswold cheese, rind removed, cut into small pieces
1 tbls chopped parsley
2 garlic cloves, crushed
salt and paprika pepper
1 tbls lemon juice
lemon wedges, to serve

Place the rice in a casserole dish. Add the boiling water, cover and microwave on **High** for 10 minutes. Drain and reserve.

Remove the mushroom stalks carefully and chop them finely. Place in a bowl with the butter and spring onions and microwave on **High** for 2 minutes. Stir in the sweetcorn, cooked rice, cheese, parsley and garlic. Season to taste.

Fill the mushroom caps with the stuffing and sprinkle with lemon juice. Arrange on a serving plate and microwave on **Medium-High** for 3-4 minutes. Rearrange after 2 minutes. The exact cooking time will depend on the firmness of the mushrooms.

Serve hot with lemon wedges and a little extra paprika.

French bean salad

SERVES 4

350 g (12 oz) French beans, topped and tailed
12 cherry tomatoes, quartered
12 black olives, stoned
chicory or chopped Chinese leaves, to serve
1 tbls sesame seeds
15 g (½ oz) butter
For the dressing
50 g (2 oz) full fat soft cheese with chives
1 tbls olive oil
2 tsp white wine vinegar
2 tbls natural yoghurt
½ tsp Dijon mustard
paprika pepper
pinch of garlic salt

Cut the beans into 4 cm (1½ inch) lengths and place in a shallow dish. Add 4 tbls water and cover with stretch film, piercing it to allow the steam to escape. Microwave on **High** for 7-8 minutes, or until just tender, stirring once. Drain and cool.

To make the dressing, place the cheese in a small bowl. Microwave on **Medium** for 30 seconds to soften. Beat in the oil, vinegar, yoghurt, mustard, paprika and garlic salt.

Toss the beans in the dressing. Add the tomatoes and olives and arrange on the salad leaves.

Place the sesame seeds and butter in a small bowl and microwave on **High** for 1 minute. Sprinkle over the salad and serve.

Variation: Use frozen French beans and cook for half the time.

Mussels in white wine

SERVES 4

1.5 kg (3 lb) live mussels, scrubbed and cleaned
2 onions, finely chopped
1 carrot, cut into thin strips
1 tbls fresh chopped or ½ tsp dried thyme
2 cloves garlic, crushed
25 g (1 oz) butter
25 g (1 oz) plain flour
600 ml (1 pint) dry white wine
salt and pepper
4 tbls single cream
1 green apple, cut into thin strips
1 tbls chopped parsley

Place the onions, carrot, thyme, garlic and butter in a large bowl and microwave on **High** for 2 minutes. Stir in the flour, then gradually mix in the wine. Microwave on **High** for 4-5 minutes, or until thickened, stirring 2 or 3 times. Season to taste.

Add the mussels and toss them in the sauce. Cover with stretch film and microwave on **High** for 4-5 minutes. Remove all open mussels with a draining spoon and keep warm. Cook any remaining mussels on **High** for 2 minutes. Discard any unopened mussels.

Remove one shell from each mussel and place the mussels in their remaining shells in a serving dish or place in the serving dish whole. Stir the cream, apple and parsley into the sauce, pour over and serve.

Serving idea: Supply an empty dish or dishes to dispose of the shells at table. Finger bowls, to prevent napkins gctting too dirty, arc also a good idea.

Variation: Replace the wine with a dry cider.

Vegetable terrine

SERVES 6

30 g (1¼ oz) packet aspic powder
300 ml (½ pint) hot weak chicken stock
50 ml (2 fl oz) dry sherry
100 g (4 oz) skimmed milk cheese or ricotta cheese
5 tbls low-calorie mayonnaise
4 tsp lemon juice
cayenne pepper
5 asparagus spears
175 g (6 oz) carrots, cut into thin sticks
100 g (4 oz) frozen petit pois
1 orange, peeled and thinly sliced
50 g (2 oz) watercress, finely chopped
fresh chervil, to garnish

Sprinkle the aspic powder over the chicken stock and leave for 5 minutes. Stir well then microwave on **High** for 2-3 minutes, or until the aspic has dissolved, stirring 2 or 3 times. Cool. Stir in the sherry.

Beat the cheese, mayonnaise, lemon juice and cayenne pepper together in a medium bowl. Gradually add the aspic liquid and blend together. Chill until the consistency is syrupy, but not set.

Meanwhile place the asparagus in a shallow dish, add 2 tbls water, cover and microwave on **High** for 3 minutes. Drain and refresh under cold running water. Prepare the carrots in the same way.

Place the petit pois in a dish and microwave on **High** for 2 minutes. Refresh under cold running water.

Rinse a 1.2 litre (2 pint) loaf tin with cold water, then arrange the orange slices over the base. Pour a quarter of the cheese mixture over. Refrigerate to set (this takes about 15 minutes). Continue with a layer of asparagus and a quarter of the cheese mixture. Refrigerate to set. Add a layer of the peas.

Combine the chopped watercress with the remaining cheese mixture. Add half to the tin and refrigerate to set. Layer with the carrots and top with more cheese and watercress mix. Refrigerate for 2 hours to set.

Loosen the edges with a knife and turn out on to a flat serving dish. Garnish and serve sliced.

Crunchy Brie triangles

SERVES 4

225 g (8 oz) slightly unripe Brie cheese
50 g (2 oz) fresh white breadcrumbs
25 g (1 oz) butter or margarine
25 g (1 oz) flaked almonds, chopped
1 tbls plain flour
1 egg, beaten
cherry tomatoes, to garnish

Cut the Brie into 8 wedges by cutting across into 3 pieces and cutting the middle piece into 3 and bottom piece into 4 triangles. Place in the freezer for one hour.

Place the breadcrumbs and butter in a bowl and microwave on **High** for 3 minutes, stirring twice. Add the almonds, stir and microwave on **High** for 2-3 minutes, stirring twice. Leave to cool.

Turn the cheese wedges in the flour to coat them all over. Dip them in the beaten egg, then coat with the browned breadcrumbs and nuts. Arrange in a circle on a roasting rack with the thickest parts to the outside.

Microwave on **Medium** for 2-2½ minutes or until heated and soft. Take care not to let it overcook. Garnish with cherry tomato halves.

Serving idea: Serve with apple slices, and crusty bread if liked.

- **Top: Mexican rounds**
- **Right: Crunchy Brie triangles**
- **Bottom: Vegetable terrine**

Mexican rounds

SERVES 4

225 g (8 oz) lean minced beef
1 onion, chopped
1 clove garlic, crushed
1 tbls vegetable oil
1 tsp chilli powder or 1 tbls chilli seasoning
2 small green chillies, finely chopped
2 tbls tomato purée
1 tsp plain flour
3 tomatoes, skinned and chopped
salt and pepper
198 g (7 oz) can red kidney beans, drained and rinsed
4 tostada shells
2 lettuce leaves, shredded
8 olives, stoned and sliced

Place the onion, garlic, oil, chilli powder or seasoning and chillies in a medium casserole dish and microwave on **High** for 2 minutes. Stir in the minced beef and microwave on **High** for 5 minutes, stirring twice.

Stir in the tomato purée, flour and chopped tomatoes. Microwave on **High** for 1-2 minutes. Season to taste, add the red kidney beans, cover and microwave on **High** for 4 minutes.

Place the tostada shells in a pile on a sheet of absorbent paper and microwave on **High** for 30-45 seconds. Arrange on 4 serving plates. Cover with the beef mixture, top with shredded lettuce and olive slices.

Variation: Serve the filling in taco shells or pitta bread. Warm the shells or pitta bread for 30 seconds on **High** before adding the filling.

Fish kebabs

SERVES 4

8 large prawns or 4 crayfish
225 g (8 oz) monkfish or huss, cut into 8 pieces
4 baby scallops, defrosted if frozen
8 lime slices
8 bay leaves
8 button mushrooms
4 tomato halves or 8 cherry tomatoes

For the marinade

1 small onion, grated
2 tbls olive oil
2 tbls lime or lemon juice
2 cloves garlic, crushed
1 tbls chopped parsley

Peel the prawns, leaving the tail attached. Thread the prawns, monkfish, scallops (halved if using larger ones), slices of lime, bay leaves and vegetables on to 4 *wooden* skewers, making sure that a piece of monkfish is at each end. Place in a shallow dish.

Mix together the marinade ingredients, pour over the kebabs and leave for 2 hours in the refrigerator. Baste 2 or 3 times.

Place the kebab sticks over a clean shallow dish with the ends supported by the edges of the dish. Microwave on **High** for 5-6 minutes, rearranging after 3 minutes. Serve.

Serving idea: Serve on a bed of long grain rice, flavoured with freshly chopped herbs.

Variation: Any combination of fish may be used. Include a smoked fish to give variety.

Devilish crab

SERVES 4

4 × 700 g (1½ lb) crabs
25 g (1 oz) butter or margarine
50 g (2 oz) button mushrooms, sliced
1 tbls plain flour
150 ml (5 fl oz) dry white wine
1 tbls chilli sauce
1 tbls tomato ketchup
½ tsp curry paste
6 spring onions, chopped
40 g (1½ oz) breadcrumbs
2 tbls double cream
50 g (2 oz) Emmenthal cheese, grated
cayenne pepper
lemon twists, to garnish

To prepare the crabs, remove the meat from the body. Discard the mouth and stomach sac and grey gills. Remove the meat from the claws and large legs. Reserve the small legs to garnish.

Using a hammer or rolling pin gently tap the edge of the shell cavity along the inside of the natural line and remove the surplus shell. Wash and dry the shells thoroughly.

Place the butter and mushrooms in a bowl and microwave on **High** for 2 minutes. Stir in the flour then gradually add the wine. Add the chilli sauce, tomato ketchup and curry paste. Microwave on **High** for 1½-2 minutes, or until thickened. Stir 2 or 3 times during cooking. Add the onions, breadcrumbs, cream and crabmeat.

Divide the mixture between the shells and sprinkle with the cheese and cayenne pepper. Arrange in a shallow dish and microwave on **High** for 3½-4 minutes, until hot and bubbly.

Garnish with the reserved legs, and lemon twists. Serve the crab immediately.

Serving idea: Place under a pre-heated grill to brown if wished. Serve with a mixed salad and brown bread.

Variation: Use canned crabmeat and serve in individual shell dishes.

- **Left: Fish kebabs**
- **Right: Devilish crab**

Orange and spinach stuffed trout

SERVES 4

4 × 175 g (6 oz) trout, cleaned
25 g (1 oz) butter or margarine
1 onion, finely chopped
175 g (6 oz) frozen chopped spinach, defrosted
50 g (2 oz) fresh brown breadcrumbs
grated rind 1 orange
1 tbls orange juice
salt and pepper
½ tsp ground nutmeg
4 orange slices, halved
4 bay leaves
lemon and orange wedges, to garnish

Place the butter and onion in a bowl and microwave on **High** for 2 minutes. Put the spinach in a sieve and press down firmly to drain off all the excess liquid. Mix well with the onions. Add the breadcrumbs and combine together with a fork to make a fairly coarse stuffing.

Add the orange rind, orange juice, seasoning and nutmeg. Fill the trout cavities with the stuffing.

Arrange the trout in a shallow dish, head next to tail. Shield the heads and tails with small pieces of smooth aluminium foil. Arrange 2 orange slices and a bay leaf on top of each fish.

Cover the dish with stretch film, pierce it and microwave on **High** for 9-10 minutes, or until tender. Rearrange after 5 minutes and remove the foil after 8 minutes.

Leave to stand for 3 minutes, remove stretch film, and garnish with lemon and orange wedges just before serving.

Variation: If wished, omit stuffing and just top with orange slices and bay leaves. Sprinkle with 2 tbls orange juice and place a knob of butter inside each cavity. Cook as above for 6-8 minutes.

• Left to right: Orange and spinach stuffed trout; Plaice rolls with mustard sauce

Plaice rolls with mustard sauce

SERVES 4

8 plaice fillets, approx 50 g (2 oz) each, skinned
50 g (2 oz) unsalted shelled peanuts, chopped
1 tbls fresh parsley, chopped
6 tbls dry white wine or vermouth
1 tbls lemon juice
salt and pepper
2 egg yolks
2 tsp French mustard
4 tbls double cream
To garnish
watercress
lemon twists

Mix the nuts and parsley together and sprinkle over the plaice fillets. Roll them up and secure each one with a wooden cocktail stick.

Place the rolls side by side in a single layer in a shallow dish. Mix the wine or vermouth with the lemon juice and seasoning. Pour over the fillets. Cover with stretch film, pierce and microwave on **High** for 3-4 minutes, or until the fish flakes when gently tested with a fine skewer.

Using a fish slice, transfer the rolls to a warmed serving dish and microwave the cooking liquor on **High** for 30 seconds, or until boiling.

Mix together the egg yolks, mustard and cream. Stir in a little of the liquor. Add to the remaining liquor and microwave on **High** for 60-90 seconds, stirring 4 or 5 times. Do not boil or the egg yolks may curdle. Pour around the fish garnished with watercress and lemon twists, and serve immediately.

Lamb with couscous

This delicious lamb stew has a slightly spicy flavour which goes well with couscous, but it tastes equally good with rice. If you are unable to buy pre-cooked packet couscous substitute with long grain rice and cook according to your manufacturer's handbook.

SERVES 4

450 g (1 lb) lamb shoulder fillet, cubed
50 g (2 oz) butter
1 tbls vegetable oil
1 onion, chopped
2 cloves garlic, crushed
1 tbls ground coriander
1 tsp paprika
1 tbls plain flour
2 leeks, sliced diagonally
2 carrots, sliced diagonally
100 g (4 oz) okra or courgettes, sliced
411 g (14½ oz) can Napolitan sauce
salt
350 g (12 oz) pre-cooked couscous
450 ml (¾ pint) warm water
rosemary sprig, to garnish

Place half the butter in a large casserole with the oil, onion and garlic. Microwave on **High** for 2 minutes. Stir in the coriander and paprika. Microwave on **High** for 1 minute.

Toss the lamb and flour together, add to the casserole and microwave on **High** for 3 minutes, stirring twice. Add the leeks, carrots, okra, sauce and seasoning. Microwave on **High** for 5 minutes. Stir well, cover and microwave on **Medium** for 30 minutes, stirring twice.

Meanwhile place the couscous in a shallow dish and sprinkle with the warm water. Leave for 10 minutes. Stir well and cover with stretch film. Pierce the film and microwave on **Medium-High** for 5 minutes, stirring twice.

Stir the remaining butter into the couscous, season to taste and arrange around the edge of a large serving plate. Place the lamb and vegetables in the centre, garnish with a sprig of rosemary and serve.

Oriental liver

SERVES 4

450 g (1 lb) lambs' liver, cut into thin strips
1 large red pepper, seeded and cut into 1 cm (½ inch) strips
2 tbls vegetable oil
2.5 cm (1 inch) piece root ginger, peeled and grated
225 g (8 oz) Savoy cabbage, shredded
100 g (4 oz) mange-tout, trimmed
8 spring onions, cut diagonally
2 tbls soy sauce
2 tbls dry sherry
spring onion curls, to garnish (optional)

Heat a large browning dish for 7 minutes, or according to the manufacturer's instructions. Meanwhile cut the red pepper strips diagonally to make diamond shapes.

Place the oil, ginger and liver in the pre-heated dish and stir well for 30 seconds. Microwave on **High** for 2 minutes, stirring twice.

Add the pepper strips, Savoy cabbage and mange-tout. Microwave on **High** for 3-4 minutes, depending on desired crispness.

Add the spring onions, soy sauce and sherry and microwave on **High** for 1 minute. Garnish with spring onion curls, if using and serve.

Variation: Add different vegetables for variety. Try carrots, bean sprouts or celery.

- **Top: Oriental liver**
- **Right: Lamb with couscous**
- **Bottom: Chicken roulades**

Chicken roulades

SERVES 4

4 boneless chicken breasts, skinned
1 clove garlic, crushed
25 g (1 oz) butter or margarine
75 g (3 oz) Cheddar cheese, grated
2 spring onions, chopped
1 tbls chopped walnuts
1 tbls toasted breadcrumbs
1 tbls fresh parsley, chopped
salt and pepper
75 g (3 oz) cream crackers, crushed
1 tsp paprika
¼ tsp cayenne pepper
2 tbls vegetable oil
1 egg, lightly beaten
chopped parsley, to garnish (optional)

Place the garlic and butter in a dish and microwave on **High** for 2 minutes, stirring twice. Add the cheese, onions, walnuts, breadcrumbs, parsley and seasoning. Mix together and set aside.

Place the chicken breasts on a wooden board and pound lightly to flatten. Divide the filling between the breasts and spread it evenly over them. Roll them up and secure with *wooden* cocktail sticks.

Mix the crackers, paprika and cayenne pepper together. Brush the rolls with the oil and coat with half the cracker mixture. Coat in beaten egg and finally with the remaining cracker mixture.

Place the rolls on a roasting rack, seam side down. Cover with absorbent paper and microwave on **High** for 7-8 minutes, or until the juices from the chicken run clear.

Remove the cocktail sticks. Serve, garnished with parsley, if using.

Serving idea: Serve with a crisp salad and new potatoes.

Variation: Lay a small slice of smoked ham on each chicken breast before spreading with the filling.

Brown rice risotto with ham

SERVES 4

350 g (12 oz) long grain brown rice
25 g (1 oz) butter or margarine
2 onions, finely chopped
900 ml (1½ pints) hot stock
4 sticks celery, sliced
1 small red pepper, seeded and chopped
100 g (4 oz) small button mushrooms, halved
100 g (4 oz) petit pois
salt and pepper
100 g (4 oz) ham, diced
100 g (4 oz) garlic sausage, thinly sliced
3 tbls fresh chopped parsley
2 tbls Parmesan cheese, grated (optional)

Place the butter and onions in a large deep bowl and microwave on **High** for 3 minutes. Add the rice and microwave on **High** for 1 minute. Add the stock and cover with stretch film. Pierce the film and microwave on **High** for 5 minutes. Reduce to **Medium** for 20 minutes.

Add the celery. Cover and microwave on **High** for 2 minutes. Add the red pepper, mushrooms and petit pois, and season to taste. Re-cover and microwave the mixture on **High** for 5 minutes.

Toss the rice mixture with a fork to separate the grains. Stir in the ham, garlic sausage, parsley, and cheese if using. Serve immediately.

Serving idea: Serve with green salad and hot garlic bread.

Variation: Replace 150 ml (5 fl oz) of the stock with dry white wine.

Vegetable rice ring

SERVES 4

225 g (8 oz) long grain rice
900 ml (1 ½ pints) boiling salted water
1 green pepper, seeded and chopped
175 g (6 oz) frozen sweetcorn, defrosted
175 g (6 oz) frozen peas, defrosted
2 tbls bottled French dressing
3-4 drops Tabasco sauce
For the filling
3-4 sticks celery, sliced
8-10 cherry tomatoes, quartered or halved
3 spring onions, chopped (optional)
1 tbls pine nuts
1 tbls bottled mustard vinaigrette
salt and pepper

Place the rice in a large deep bowl. Add the boiling water and cover with stretch film. Pierce the film and microwave on **High** for 10 minutes.

Rinse the rice under cold running water, drain and place in a clean bowl. Add the pepper, sweetcorn, peas, French dressing and Tabasco. Stir well and place in a 1.2 litre (2 pint) ring mould. Press down and smooth the surface with the back of a spoon. Cover and leave until cold.

Turn the rice ring out on to a serving dish. Mix together the filling ingredients, season to taste and arrange in the centre of the ring.

Serving idea: Turn out the ring on to a bed of salad leaves.

Variations: Add diced continental sausage, salami or flaked tuna to the filling ingredients.

- **Top: Vegetable rice ring**
- **Left: Brown rice risotto with ham**
- **Bottom: Seafood spaghetti**

Seafood spaghetti

SERVES 4

225 g (8 oz) spaghetti
1.7 litres (3 pints) boiling salted water
1 tbls vegetable oil
25 g (1 oz) butter or margarine
salt and pepper
For the sauce
100 g (4 oz) baby scallops
150 ml (¼ pint) dry white wine
100 g (4 oz) skimmed milk or ricotta cheese
2 egg yolks
1 tbls tomato purée
6 spring onions, chopped
100 g (4 oz) peeled prawns
100 g (4 oz) mussels, shelled
90 g (3½ oz) can tuna in brine, drained and flaked
salt and pepper
2-3 drops Tabasco sauce
2 tbls freshly chopped dill
2 unshelled prawns, to garnish (optional)

Place the spaghetti in a large deep bowl with the water and oil. Cover with stretch film. Pierce the film and microwave on **High** for 5 minutes. Leave to stand.

Pierce the scallops with a skewer and place them with the wine in a shallow dish. Cover with stretch film. Pierce the film and microwave on **High** for 3 minutes. Strain the scallops, reserving the wine.

Mix the cheese, egg yolks, tomato purée and wine together. Microwave on **High** for 3-4 minutes, or until thickened, stirring 3 or 4 times.

Stir in the onions, prawns, mussels, tuna and scallops. Season to taste and microwave on **High** for 2 minutes, to heat through, stirring 2 or 3 times. Stir in the Tabasco and dill and garnish with prawns, if using.

Drain the spaghetti, toss it in butter and season to taste. Place in a deep serving dish, spoon over the sauce and serve.

Fennel Provençal

SERVES 4 as an accompaniment or 2 as a main course

2 fennel bulbs, halved lengthways
2 tbls lemon juice
4 tbls water
fennel leaves, to garnish
For the sauce
1 onion, chopped
1 clove garlic, crushed
1 tbls vegetable oil
400 g (14 oz) can chopped tomatoes
salt and pepper
For the topping
25 g (1 oz) butter or margarine
25 g (1 oz) breadcrumbs
50 g (2 oz) mature Cheddar cheese, grated

To make the sauce, place the onion, garlic and oil in a 1.2 litre (2 pint) casserole dish and microwave on **High** for 2 minutes. Add the tomatoes, stir and microwave on **High** for 7 minutes, stirring twice. Season to taste, cover and set aside.

Place the fennel in a single layer in a shallow dish with the lemon juice and water. Cover with stretch film. Pierce the film and microwave on **High** for 8-9 minutes or until the fennel is just tender. Stir once in the middle of cooking.

Drain the fennel and return it to the dish. Spoon over the sauce.

To make the topping, place the butter and breadcrumbs on a shallow dish and microwave on **High** for 2-3 minutes, or until golden, stirring 2 or 3 times. Sprinkle the fennel with cheese and microwave on **High** for 1½ minutes, or until the cheese has melted. Sprinkle with toasted breadcrumbs and serve garnished with fennel leaves.

Variation: Use celery hearts instead of fennel. A combination of vegetables can also be served with the Provençal sauce. Courgettes, aubergines, onions and mushrooms go together well.

Vegetable casserole

SERVES 4 as an accompaniment or 2 as a vegetarian main course.

25 g (1 oz) butter or margarine
1-2 tbls ground coriander
2-3 tsp ground cumin
2 tsp paprika
200 ml (7 fl oz) hot vegetable stock
1 tbls tomato purée
1 kohlrabi, peeled, quartered and thinly sliced
350 g (12 oz) leeks, sliced
175 g (6 oz) broccoli florets
1 red pepper, seeded and cut into thin strips
400 g (14 oz) can artichoke hearts, drained
½ × 400 g (14 oz) can chick peas, drained

Place the butter and spices in a large casserole dish and microwave on **High** for 1 minute, stirring after 30 seconds. Stir in the stock, tomato purée, kohlrabi, and leeks. Cover and microwave on **High** for 4 minutes. Add the broccoli, re-cover and microwave on **High** for 4 minutes.

Stir in the red pepper, artichoke hearts and chick peas. Re-cover and microwave on **Medium-High** for 7-8 minutes, stirring twice.

Serve with cheese topped croûtons.

Vegetables en papillote

SERVES 4 as an accompaniment or 2 as a vegetarian main course

2 courgettes, cut into matchstick strips
3 carrots, cut into matchstick strips
½ red pepper, seeded and cut into matchstick strips
½ green pepper, seeded and cut into matchstick strips
100 g (4 oz) beansprouts
2 tbls lemon juice
1 tbls freshly chopped mixed herbs
salt and pepper

• **Fennel Provençal; Vegetables en papillote; Vegetable casserole**

Mix the vegetables together and divide them between 4 30 cm (12 inch) × 15cm (6 inch) rectangles of baking parchment. Mix the lemon juice, herbs and seasoning together and pour over. Fold the paper over to make squares and fold back the edges to make neat parcels.

Place the parcels on a large plate and microwave on **High** for 6-8 minutes, depending on desired crispness. Shake gently after 5 minutes. Serve the vegetables in their 'parcels', cutting each diagonally from corner to corner to open. Alternatively decant onto individual plates.

Rhubarb and banana fool

SERVES 4

400 g (14 oz) rhubarb, cut into 2.5 cm (1 inch) pieces
40 g (1½ oz) granulated sugar
150 ml (5 fl oz) milk
1 tbls cornflour
1 tbls caster sugar
4-5 drops vanilla essence
2-3 drops pink food colour, optional
1 large banana
1 tsp lemon juice
142 ml (5 fl oz) carton double cream, whipped

Place the rhubarb in a shallow dish and sprinkle with the granulated sugar and 3 tbls water. Cover with stretch film, pierce, and microwave on **High** for 6-8 minutes, depending on the tenderness of the rhubarb.

Place the rhubarb in a food processor or liquidizer and purée. Cover and leave to cool.

To make a 'custard', mix 2 tbls of the milk with the cornflour and caster sugar in a jug. Add the milk to the jug and microwave on **High** for 1½ minutes, or until nearly boiling. Stir well, and microwave on **High** for 1 minute, to thicken. Stir 2 or 3 times.

Add the vanilla essence to the 'custard'. Mix into the fruit purée and add a few drops of colouring, if wished. Cover, set aside and leave until cold.

Place the banana and lemon juice in a food processor or blender and purée. Mix into the rhubarb custard. Swirl in the cream to give a marbled effect and serve in 4 individual glasses.

Serving idea: Serve with dessert biscuits.

Variation: Use 250 ml (8 fl oz) thick set natural yoghurt instead of cream for a sharper dessert.

Use a 524 g (1 lb 3 oz) can rhubarb, drained. Omit the sugar and do not cook.

Zabaglione with grapes

SERVES 4

50 g (2 oz) small black grapes, halved and seeded
50 g (2 oz) small green grapes, halved and seeded
1 egg
3 egg yolks
40 g (1½ oz) caster sugar
50 ml (2 fl oz) Marsala

Mix the grapes together and set aside. Place the egg, egg yolks and sugar in a large bowl and whisk until thick and frothy.

Place the Marsala in a small bowl and microwave on **High** for 1 minute. Pour on to the eggs, whisking continuously. Microwave the mix on **Medium** for 1½-2 minutes.

Whisk with an electric mixer for 3 minutes, then microwave on **Medium** for 1 minute. Pour into 4 glasses, place the grapes on top and allow them to sink into the zabaglione. Serve immediately.

Serving idea: Decorate the side of each glass with a bunch of frosted grapes. Serve with sponge biscuits.

Variation: Replace the Marsala with Madeira or sweet sherry.

Butterscotch ice cream

SERVES 4

50 g (2 oz) butter
2 tbls golden syrup
50 g (2 oz) light muscovado sugar
2 tbls water
1 egg yolk
284 ml (10 fl oz) carton whipping cream, whipped
flaked almonds (optional)

Place the butter, syrup and sugar in a 1.7 litre (3 pint) bowl and microwave on **High** for 2 minutes, stirring twice to dissolve the sugar. Microwave on **High** for a further 2 minutes. Cautiously stir in the water. It may splatter, so take care. Beat in the egg yolk and leave to cool.

Fold the mixture into the cream so that it is well incorporated and transfer to a freezer-proof container. Freeze until firm, about 4-5 hours.

If using, place the almonds on a plate and microwave on **High** for 2½-3 minutes, or until lightly browned, stirring 3 or 4 times. Cool.

Serve in scoops, topped with almonds if using. Accompany with wafers, if liked.

Variation: Stir in 25 g (1 oz) chopped glacé cherries before freezing.

• Zabaglione with grapes; Rhubarb and banana fool; Butterscotch ice cream

● **Autumn pudding; Raspberry and walnut surprise; Vanilla and mocha castles**

Autumn pudding

SERVES 4-6

225 g (8 oz) plums, stoned and coarsely chopped
175 g (6 oz) greengages, stoned and coarsely chopped
1 pear, cored and diced
225 g (8 oz) blackberries or raspberries
100 g (4 oz) caster sugar
7-8 slices brown or white bread, crusts removed
fresh fruit and currant leaf, to decorate

Place the fruit in a casserole dish and sprinkle with the sugar. Stir well, cover and microwave on **High** for 4 minutes. Stir and microwave on **High** for a further 1-2 minutes, or until the fruit has just softened.

Line the base and sides of a 900 ml (1½ pint) pudding basin with slices of bread, ensuring that there are no spaces between the slices. Reserve enough bread to make a lid.

Place the fruit and any juice in the basin and cover with the remaining bread. Place a saucer on top and top with a heavy weight. Leave overnight to chill and for the juice to soak into the bread.

To serve, turn out on to a plate and decorate the top of the pudding with fruit and leaves.

Variation: Any combination of fruits can be used.

Vanilla and mocha castles

SERVES 4

50 g (2 oz) plain flour
¼ tsp salt
½ tsp baking powder
1 tbls cocoa powder
50 g (2 oz) soft margarine
50 g (2 oz) caster sugar
1 egg, beaten
1 tsp coffee granules dissolved in 2 tbls boiling water
grated chocolate, to decorate
For the vanilla sauce
1 tbls cornflour
1 tbls caster sugar
250 ml (8 fl oz) milk
3-4 drops vanilla essence
pinch of grated nutmeg

Make the sauce first. Blend the cornflour and sugar together with a little milk. Place the remaining milk in a jug and microwave on **High** for 1½-2 minutes, until almost boiling.

Pour the milk on to the cornflour mixture and stir well. Microwave on **High** for 1 minute, to thicken, stirring 2 or 3 times. Stir in the vanilla essence and nutmeg, cover and set aside.

Sift the flour, salt, baking powder and cocoa powder together into a medium bowl. Add the margarine, sugar, egg and coffee. Beat together for 2-3 minutes.

Lightly grease 4 paper drinking cups and divide the mixture between them. Microwave on **High** for 1¾-2¼ minutes or until barely dry on top. Stand for 1 minute then carefully loosen the edges and turn out on to a serving plate.

Pour a little sauce over each castle, sprinkle with grated chocolate and serve.

Variation: Serve with a chocolate sauce, made by incorporating cocoa powder or melted chocolate to taste with the vanilla sauce.

Raspberry and walnut surprise

SERVES 6

For the base
150 g (5 oz) digestive biscuits, crushed
50 g (2 oz) walnuts, finely chopped
50 g (2 oz) butter or margarine, cut into pieces
For the filling
50 g (2 oz) caster sugar
175 g (6 oz) curd cheese
2 tsp cornflour
3 eggs
3-4 drops vanilla essence
142 ml (5 fl oz) carton double cream
142 ml (5 fl oz) carton soured cream
For the decoration
100 g (4 oz) raspberries
50 g (2 oz) walnut quarters

Line the base of a 20 cm (8 inch) spring-form round tin with baking parchment or greaseproof paper.

Mix the biscuits and walnuts together. Place the butter in a small bowl and microwave on **Medium-High** for 1 minute, until melted. Stir into the biscuit mixture.

Press the mixture firmly into the prepared tin with the back of a spoon and leave to chill.

Beat the caster sugar, curd cheese and cornflour together in a 1.8-2.4 litre (3-4 pint) mixing bowl. Mix in the eggs, vanilla essence and both cartons of cream. Microwave on **High** for 3 minutes. Reduce to **Medium** for 2-3 minutes, or until thickened, whisking every 45-60 seconds. When properly thickened the mixture will hold the trail left by the whisk. Do not overcook or the mixture will separate.

Pour into the prepared tin and chill for 2-3 hours. Carefully remove from the tin and transfer to a serving plate. Decorate with raspberries and walnuts just before serving.

Choc-nut fondue

SERVES 4-6

50 g (2 oz) flaked almonds
150 g (6 oz) plain dessert chocolate, broken into pieces
250 ml (8 fl oz) whipping cream
2-3 drops vanilla essence
2 tbls rum or brandy
To serve
sponge fingers (optional)
Madeira or fruit cake, cubed
orange segments
grapes, seeded and halved
strawberries, halved
fresh pineapple chunks

Place the almonds on a plate and microwave on **High** for 3-4 minutes, or until lightly browned, stirring 2 or 3 times.

Place the chocolate and cream in a ceramic fondue dish or heatproof glass dish and microwave on **Medium-High** for 2 minutes, or until the chocolate melts. Stir the mixture 2 or 3 times during cooking.

Stir in the vanilla essence, rum or brandy and toasted almonds. Serve with a selection of dippers such as sponge fingers, cake cubes and fresh fruits.

Variation: Reserve 2 tbls of the cream and swirl it into the fondue just before serving.

Peaches in white wine

SERVES 4

4 large peaches
3 tbls golden syrup
3 sticks cinnamon
2 strips pared lemon rind
2 strips pared orange rind
150 ml (5 fl oz) dry white wine
2 tbls Grenadine
100 g (4 oz) fresh raspberries
scented geranium leaves, to decorate

Place the golden syrup in a small casserole dish with 120 ml (4 fl oz) and water stir to dissolve. Add the cinnamon, lemon and orange rind and microwave on **High** for 2 minutes. Add the wine and Grenadine.

Lower the peaches into the syrup and baste. Cover and microwave on **High** for 5-6 minutes or until soft but not mushy.

Remove peaches from the syrup with a slotted spoon. Microwave the syrup uncovered on **High** for 5 minutes. Allow the peaches to cool a little. Hold each one gently and peel off the skins with your fingers. Cut the peaches in half.

Arrange the fruit in a shallow glass dish with the raspberries. Spoon over the syrup and leave to cool. Chill the peaches, and decorate before serving.

Serving idea: Serve with freshly whipped cream or natural yoghurt.

- **Left: Choc-nut fondue**
- **Right: Peaches in white wine**

COMBINATION
STARTERS AND SNACKS

Pizza triangles

SERVES 4

175 g (6 oz) strong plain flour
1 tsp salt
2 tsp easy-blend dried yeast
120 ml (4 fl oz) tepid milk
1 tbls vegetable oil
225 g (8 oz) can chopped tomatoes, drained
1 tsp dried oregano
4 slices green pepper, halved
8 slices Hungarian salami
75 g (3 oz) Mozzarella cheese, grated
salt and pepper

Place the flour, salt and yeast in a bowl. Add the milk and oil and mix together. Knead for 5-10 minutes to make a smooth dough.

Place in a clean bowl, cover with a cloth and leave in a warm place to rise. To speed up the rising process, microwave on **High** for 15 seconds, then leave to stand for 10 minutes. Repeat once or twice more. Leave until the dough has doubled in size.

Roll out into a 20 cm (8 inch) square and cut diagonally into 4 triangles.

Place the triangles on the turntable and spread each one with the tomatoes. Sprinkle with oregano and top with slices of pepper, salami and cheese. Season to taste. Cook on **combination 250°C/30% microwave** for 20 minutes.

Microwave plus conventional
Prepare as above and microwave on **High** for 6-7 minutes. To brown, place under a pre-heated grill. Alternatively, cook in the microwave on a preheated browning dish or pizza browner.

Cheese soufflés

SERVES 6

15 g (½ oz) margarine
40 g (1½ oz) fine dry breadcrumbs
25 g (1 oz) butter
25 g (1 oz) plain flour
150 ml (5 fl oz) milk
3 eggs, separated
50 g (2 oz) Double Gloucester cheese, grated
50 g (2 oz) Cheddar cheese, grated
1 tbls chives, chopped
1 tbls French mustard
salt and paprika pepper

Preheat the oven on convection to 220°C. Grease the insides of 6 × 150 ml (5 fl oz) ramekin dishes with the margarine and coat the insides with breadcrumbs. Chill.

Place the butter in a 1.7 litre (3 pint) bowl and microwave on **High** for 30-40 seconds to melt. Stir in the flour, then gradually add the milk, stirring continuously. Microwave on **High** for 2-3 minutes, stirring 2 or 3 times. Stir in the egg yolks, cheeses, chives, mustard and seasoning.

Whisk the egg whites until stiff, then carefully fold them into the cheese sauce.

Pour the mixture into the prepared dishes, place on the wire rack and cook on **combination 220°C/10% microwave** for 9-10 minutes, or until risen and golden.

Note: This dish can only be cooked in combination in a *simultaneous* combination cooker, and cannot be cooked by microwave only.

Jacket eggs

SERVES 4

4 × 225 g (8 oz) potatoes, unpeeled, scrubbed and pricked
salt and pepper
25 g (1 oz) butter or margarine
2 tsp milk
75 g (3 oz) Cheddar cheese, grated
4 rashers streaky bacon, chopped
4 eggs
snipped chives, to garnish

Rub the potatoes with salt and place on the wire rack.

Microwave on **High** for 7 minutes, then cook on **combination 250°C/ 30% microwave** for 20 minutes or until the skins are browned.

Remove a thin slice from the top of each potato. Take out the soft centres with a spoon and place in a bowl. Mix with the butter, milk and 50 g (2 oz) of the cheese. Season.

Place the bacon in a shallow dish and microwave on **High** for 3 minutes, stirring twice. Stir into the potato mixture.

Pile the mixture back into the potato shells leaving a large hollow in the centre of each. Carefully break an egg into each hollow. Prick the yolks with a cocktail stick and sprinkle with the remaining cheese. Place on the turntable and microwave on **High** for 4-5 minutes, or until the yolks have just started to set. Sprinkle with chives and serve.

Microwave plus conventional
Place the potatoes on the turntable and microwave on **High** for 14-16 minutes or until barely tender when pricked with a skewer. Place in a preheated oven at 200°C, 400°F, Gas Mark 6 for 20 minutes to finish cooking and crisp. Finish as above.

• **Jacket eggs; Pizza triangles; Cheese soufflés**

Smoked haddock strudel

SERVES 6

For the strudel pastry
225 g (8 oz) plain flour
pinch of salt
2 tsp oil
1 egg
75 ml (3 fl oz) warm water
25 g (1 oz) butter, melted
cracked wheat, to sprinkle (optional)
For the filling
450 g (1 lb) smoked haddock
2 hard-boiled eggs, chopped
6 tbls white breadcrumbs
25 g (1 oz) margarine or butter
25 g (1 oz) plain flour
150 ml (1/4 pint) semi-skimmed milk
salt and cayenne pepper
To garnish
curly endive
lemon twists

To make the pastry, sift the flour and salt together into a bowl. Mix the oil, egg and water together. Add to the flour and beat to a soft dough. Cover with stretch film and leave for 15 minutes in a warm place.

Meanwhile prepare the filling. Place the fish in a shallow dish. Cover with stretch film, pierce the film and microwave on **High** for 3 minutes. Drain, skin, bone and flake the fish. Stir in the eggs and breadcrumbs.

Place the margarine in a jug and microwave on **High** for 30 seconds, to melt. Stir in the flour, then gradually add the milk. Microwave on **High** for 1-2 minutes or until thickened, stirring 3 or 4 times. Season to taste and mix with the fish. Leave to cool.

Preheat the oven on convection to 230°C. Roll out the dough on a lightly floured cloth until it forms a large paper-thin rectangle. Gently lift the dough and cloth together and stretch the dough using the backs of your hands, to pull the dough gradually from the centre to the outside. As the sheet of dough becomes thinner, take care not to pull holes in it. Trim the edges. Brush the pastry with half the melted butter. Spread the filling over the dough and roll up lengthways.

Place on the turn-table, curving the roll if necessary. Brush with the remaining butter and sprinkle with cracked wheat, if using.

Cook on **combination 230°C/10% microwave** for 20 minutes.

Garnish with curly endive and lemon twists before serving.

Microwave plus conventional
Prepare as above. Microwave on **High** for 7-8 minutes. Place under a preheated grill to brown, if wished.

Serving idea: Serve sliced, garnished with a selection of salad ingredients.

Seafood vol-au-vents

SERVES 4 as a starter or 2 as a snack

4 frozen medium vol-au-vents
beaten egg, to glaze
For the filling
3 tbls low-calorie mayonnaise
1 tsp tomato purée
2-3 drops Worcestershire sauce
pinch cayenne pepper
43 g (1 1/2 oz) can dressed crab
50 g (2 oz) peeled shrimps
To garnish
dill sprigs
whole shrimps

Place the vol-au-vents on the turntable. Brush with beaten egg and cook on **combination 250°C/10% microwave** for 10-12 minutes, or until golden. Place on a cooling rack, remove the lids and leave to cool.

Mix together the filling ingredients and spoon into the vol-au-vents. Top with the lid and garnish with dill and unpeeled shrimps.

• **Smoked haddock strudel; Seafood vol-au-vents**

Microwave plus conventional
Place the vol-au-vents, unglazed, upside down on a sheet of absorbent kitchen paper and place on the turntable. Microwave on **High** for $2\frac{1}{2}$-$2\frac{3}{4}$ minutes or until the vol-au-vents stay risen when the oven door is opened.

Turn up the correct way, remove the lids and leave to cool. Fill and serve as above.

Note: Cooking the vol-au-vents upside down in the microwave helps to brown the tops. However they will not be as well formed when cooked by microwave only, so it is only worth doing if speed is particularly important.

Pastry-topped onion soup

SERVES 4

3 Spanish onions, finely sliced
25 g (1 oz) butter or margarine
1-2 tbls olive oil
750 ml (1¾ pints) hot beef stock
salt and pepper
175 g (6 oz) frozen puff pastry, defrosted
2 tbls Parmesan cheese, grated
50 g (2 oz) Emmenthal cheese, grated
milk for glazing

Place the onions, butter and oil in a casserole dish. Cook on **combination 230°C/30% microwave** for 10 minutes, stirring 3 times.

Add the stock, cover and microwave on **High** for 8 minutes. Season to taste. Remove and leave to cool for 30 minutes.

Meanwhile roll the pastry out away from you into an oblong. Sprinkle with half the Parmesan cheese, fold the top third over the middle and the bottom third over both. Seal the edges.

Turn the pastry a quarter turn, re-roll, sprinkle with the remaining Parmesan cheese and fold again as before. Chill for 15 minutes.

Take 4 deep, heatproof 300 ml (½ pint) soup bowls. Roll out the pastry and cut out 4 circles slightly larger than the tops of the bowls. Reserve the trimmings.

Using a slotted spoon, lift the onions out of the stock and divide them between the 4 bowls. Sprinkle with Emmenthal cheese and add the onion soup stock.

Brush the underside of the edges of the pastry circles with water and place over the soup bowls. Press the edges on to the rims. Decorate the centres with leaves cut from the pastry trimmings. Make a small hole in the centres for the steam to escape. Brush with a little milk.

Place on the low rack and cook on **combination 230°C/10% microwave** for 16-18 minutes.

Variation: Add 2-3 tablespoons of red wine or brandy to the soup before topping with pastry.

Pâté baskets

SERVES 4

For the pâté
175 g (6 oz) chicken livers, chopped
25 g (1 oz) butter or margarine
1 small onion, chopped
1 clove garlic, crushed
1 tbls single cream
1 tbls tomato purée
1 tbls freshly chopped parsley
2 tbls fine breadcrumbs
¼ tsp ground nutmeg
salt and pepper
For the baskets
4 thin square slices brown bread, buttered lightly on both sides
To garnish
baby tomato wedges
parsley sprigs
cucumber slices

Place the butter or margarine, onion and garlic in a casserole dish and cook on **combination 250°C/30% microwave** for 4 minutes. Add the livers, stir and cook on **combination 250°C/30% microwave** for 10-15 minutes until cooked to taste. Stir twice.

Drain off any excess fat.

Purée in a blender or food processor, then add the cream, tomato purée, parsley, breadcrumbs and nutmeg. Season to taste. Mix well and chill in the refrigerator until required.

Cut the crusts off the slices of bread and press them into 4 small ramekin dishes. Cook on **combination 250°C/10% microwave** for 10 minutes or until the bread is crisp and the tops are slightly browned. If wished, remove from ramekins, place back in oven upside down for a further 1-2 minutes to crisp up the bottoms. Leave to cool.

Spoon the pâté into the baskets just before serving. Place on individual plates and garnish.

Microwave plus conventional
To make the pâté, place the butter, onion and garlic in a casserole dish and microwave on **High** for 3 minutes. Add the livers, cover and cook on **Medium** for 6 minutes, stirring twice. Finish as above.

To make the baskets, bake in a preheated oven at 180°C, 350°F, Gas Mark 4 for 15-20 minutes. Fill and serve as above.

- **Left: Pastry-topped onion soup**
- **Right: Pâté baskets**

Garlic roast beef with Yorkshire puddings

SERVES 4-6

1.5 kg (3 lb) rolled topside or sirloin of beef
2 cloves garlic, cut into slivers
salt and pepper
2 tsp cornflour
150 ml (5 fl oz) hot beef stock
For the marinade
3 tbls olive oil
1 small onion, finely chopped
1 tbls red wine vinegar
150 ml (5 fl oz) dry red wine
1 bay leaf, crumbled
For the Yorkshire puddings
50 g (2 oz) plain flour
pinch of salt
150 ml (1/4 pint) milk
1 egg

Make small slits over the beef, using a sharp knife. Insert the slivers of garlic into the slits. Rub the meat with salt and pepper.

To make the marinade, mix together the oil, onion and vinegar. Add the wine and bayleaf.

Place the beef in a deep, close-fitting dish and pour over the marinade. Cover and leave for at least 4 hours, but preferably overnight. Baste 2 or 3 times.

Remove the meat from the marinade, and place on the low wire rack over a shallow heatproof dish. Reserve the marinade. Cook the meat on **combination 200°C/30% microwave** for 25 minutes.

Meanwhile, make the batter for the Yorkshire puddings. Place the flour and salt in a mixing bowl and gradually add the milk and egg. Whisk to a smooth consistency.

Remove the meat from the rack and place it in the cooking dish. Pour over the marinade and return the meat to the oven to cook on **combination 200°C/30% microwave** for a further 15-25 minutes according to taste. Remove from the oven and cover loosely with foil.

To make the Yorkshire puddings, set the oven to heat to 250°C, on convection, and place a lightly greased patty tin or 8 ramekin dishes inside to heat for 2 minutes. Three-quarters fill the dishes or tin with batter and cook on **combination 250°C/30% microwave** for 11-12 minutes.

To make a sauce, drain off the meat juices into a jug and blend with the cornflour and hot beef stock. Season to taste and microwave on **High** for 1-2 minutes.

Note: The roast beef can be cooked in an ordinary microwave or by *sequence* combination. Consult your manufacturer's handbook for timings. The Yorkshire puddings can only be cooked by *simultaneous* combination or conventionally.

Minted lamb noisettes

SERVES 4

8 × 75 g (3 oz) lean lamb noisettes or 4 × 175 g (6 oz) leg steaks, brushed with oil
2 tbls chopped fresh mint
175 g (6 oz) button mushrooms, sliced
6 tbls lamb stock
1 tbls tomato purée
salt and pepper
1 tsp cornflour, mixed with 2 tsps water
mint sprigs, to garnish

• **Garlic roast beef with Yorkshire puddings; Minted lamb noisettes**

Trim the meat of any fat.

Place the lamb in a shallow dish and cook on **combination 250°C/10% microwave** for 10 minutes turning once during cooking time.

Mix the mint, mushrooms, stock, tomato purée and seasoning together. Pour around the lamb and cook on **combination 250°C/30% microwave** for 15-20 minutes.

Lift the lamb and mushrooms out of the cooking dish with a slotted spoon and transfer to a warmed serving plate. Add the cornflour paste to the sauce and microwave on **High** for 1 minute to thicken. Pour over the lamb and serve garnished with sprigs of mint.

Microwave plus conventional

Place the lamb in a dish and microwave on **High** for 3 minutes. Mix the sauce ingredients together, pour over the lamb and microwave on **High** for 5 minutes. Thicken the sauce and serve as above.

Honeyed ribs

SERVES 4

1.5 kg (3 lb) spare ribs
2 onions, sliced
1 clove garlic, crushed
1 tbls vegetable oil
2 tbls tomato purée
¼ tsp mild chilli powder
4 tbls clear honey
1 tbls French mustard
1 tsp powdered ginger
1 tsp cornflour
2 tbls malt vinegar
150 ml (¼ pint) beef stock
1 small green pepper, seeded and finely sliced
227 g (8 oz) can pineapple rings, drained
spring onion stems, to garnish

Place the ribs in a large shallow heatproof dish and cook on **combination 250°C/30% microwave** for 15-20 minutes. Drain.

Place the onions, garlic and oil in a dish. Microwave on **High** for 3 minutes. Add the tomato purée, chilli powder, honey, mustard and ginger and blend together. In a jug, blend the cornflour with the vinegar and stock. Add to the onions and stir in well. Microwave on **High** for 3 minutes, stirring twice. Reduce to **Medium** for 3 minutes.

Add the green pepper to the sauce and spoon over the ribs. Cook on **combination 200°C/10% microwave** for 25-30 minutes, basting occasionally.

Cut the pineapple rings into small pieces and add to the sauce. Stir well and cook on **combination 200°C/10% microwave** for a further 10 minutes.

Garnish with spring onions and serve.

Microwave plus conventional
Place the ribs in a large shallow dish. Cover with a sheet of greaseproof paper and microwave on **High** for 5 minutes. Drain off excess fat.

Prepare the sauce as above and pour over the ribs. Turn the ribs to coat them well and microwave uncovered on **High** for 10 minutes. Reduce to **Medium-Low** for 10 minutes. Baste 3 or 4 times.

Add the pineapple, stir well and microwave on **High** for 5 minutes. Serve as above.

Savoury pork and apple plait

SERVES 6

450 g (1 lb) pork sausagemeat
2 onions, finely chopped
1 large green eating apple, cored and grated
2 tsp fresh mixed herbs, chopped
1 tsp made English mustard
salt and pepper
400 g (14 oz) puff pastry, defrosted if frozen
1 egg, beaten
sesame seeds for sprinkling
apple slices and parsley, to garnish

Mix the sausagemeat, onions, apple, herbs, mustard and seasoning together. Form into a neat roll.

Roll out the pastry to a rectangle 33 × 28 cm (13 × 11 inches). Trim the edges. Lightly mark the rectangle into three lengthways. Place the sausagemeat down the centre.

Make diagonal cuts 2.5 cm (1 inch) apart along the uncovered pastry, to within 1 cm (½ inch) of the filling. Brush with a little egg and fold the flaps of pastry over the sausagemeat alternately like a plait.

Brush the plait with the remaining egg, sprinkle with sesame seeds and cook on **combination 200°C/30% microwave** for 25-30 minutes. Garnish before serving.

- **Top: Savoury pork and apple plait**
- **Right: Chicken and pepper pie**
- **Bottom: Honeyed ribs**

Chicken and pepper pie

SERVES 4

700 g (1½ lb) potatoes, cubed
4 tbls water
50 g (2 oz) butter or margarine
salt and pepper
6 rashers streaky bacon, chopped
2 small onions, thinly sliced
1 green pepper, cored, seeded and chopped
1 red pepper, cored, seeded and chopped
1 yellow pepper, cored, seeded and chopped
40 g (1½ oz) plain flour
250 ml (8 fl oz) hot chicken stock
450 g (1 lb) chicken breasts, diced
2 green chillies, seeded and finely chopped

Place the potatoes in a shallow dish with the water and cover with stretch film. Pierce the film and microwave on **High** for 10-12 minutes stirring once, until the potatoes are soft when pricked with a skewer. Drain and mash with half the butter. Season to taste.

Place the bacon in a large oval casserole and microwave on **High** for 3 minutes, stirring twice. Add the remaining butter, the onions and peppers and microwave on **High** for 5 minutes. Stir in the flour and microwave on **High** for 2 minutes, then gradually add the stock and microwave on **High** for 3 minutes, stirring twice. Stir in the chicken, and chillies.

Cover with a lid and cook on **combination 250°C/30% microwave** for 20 minutes. Season to taste.

Pipe or spoon the potato on top and cook on **combination 250°C/10% microwave** for 25-30 minutes.

Microwave plus conventional
Cook potato and prepare filling as above. To cook, microwave on **Medium** for 15-18 minutes, stirring twice. Top with potato and microwave on **Medium** for 10 minutes. Place under a preheated grill to brown.

Smoked fish cobbler

SERVES 4

450 g (1 lb) smoked cod, skinned and cut into 2.5 cm (1 inch) pieces
225 g (8 oz) smoked mackerel, skinned and cut into 2.5 cm (1 inch) pieces
25 g (1 oz) butter or margarine
25 g (1 oz) plain flour
300 ml (½ pint) milk
salt and pepper
½ tsp dry mustard
50 g (2 oz) mature Cheddar cheese, grated
100 g (4 oz) frozen peas

For the topping

175 g (6 oz) granary malted brown flour
3 tsp baking powder
salt and paprika pepper
40 g (1½ oz) butter or margarine
100-120 ml (3½-4 fl oz) milk
milk for glazing

Place the cod in a shallow dish and cover with stretch film. Pierce the film and microwave on **High** for 2½-3 minutes. Drain the cod, mix with the mackerel, and place in a 9 cm (3½ inch) heatproof dish.

Place the butter in a bowl and microwave on **High** for 30 seconds. Stir in the flour, then gradually add the milk. Microwave on **High** for 3 minutes or until thickened, stirring 3 or 4 times. Season with salt, pepper and mustard.

Stir the cheese and frozen peas into the sauce and pour over the fish.

Preheat the oven on convection to 250°C. To make the topping, mix the flour, baking powder and seasoning together in a bowl. Rub in the margarine. Add sufficient milk to mix to a soft dough.

Roll the dough out, on a floured surface, to 2 cm (¾ inch) thick and cut into 3 cm (1¼ inch) rounds.

Arrange the rounds in a circle on top of the fish. Brush with milk to glaze. Cook on **combination 250°C/ 30% microwave** for 12 minutes or until the topping is browned.

Microwave plus conventional

Prepare as above and microwave on **High** for 6-7 minutes, or until the dough springs back when lightly pressed. If wished, place under a preheated grill to brown.

Prawn gougère

SERVES 4-6

For the choux pastry
150 ml (¼ pint) water
50 g (2 oz) butter or margarine
65 g (2½ oz) plain flour
3 eggs, beaten
salt and pepper
For the filling
225 g (8 oz) peeled prawns, drained
25 g (1 oz) butter or margarine
1 onion, sliced
25 g (1 oz) plain flour
300 ml (½ pint) skimmed milk
1 tbls parsley, chopped
3 tomatoes, skinned and chopped
1 tbls Parmesan cheese, grated
1 tbls brown breadcrumbs
To garnish
3 unpeeled prawns
3 half lemon slices

To make the pastry, place the water and butter in a large bowl and microwave on **High** for 3 minutes, or until boiling. Stir in the flour. Microwave on **High** for 45 seconds. Beat in the eggs and seasoning.

Pipe or spoon the pastry mixture around the edge of a well-greased 23 cm (9 inch) flan dish.

To make the filling, place the butter and onion in a casserole dish and microwave on **High** for 2 minutes. Stir in the flour, then gradually add the milk. Microwave on **High** for 3-4 minutes, or until thickened, stirring 3 or 4 times. Stir in the parsley, tomatoes and prawns.

Season to taste and pour into the centre of the flan dish. Mix the Parmesan cheese and breadcrumbs together and sprinkle over. Place on the wire rack and cook on **combination 250°C/30% microwave** for 20-25 minutes or until brown. Garnish with whole prawns and lemon slices, and serve.

• **Left: Smoked fish cobbler; Right: Prawn gougère**

Dauphinoise vegetables

SERVES 2 as a main course or 4 as a starter

400 g (14 oz) potatoes, peeled and thinly sliced
4 tbls water
15 g (½ oz) butter
1 clove garlic, crushed
salt and pepper
¼ tsp freshly ground nutmeg
142 ml (5 fl oz) carton single cream
2 onions, thinly sliced
175 g (6 oz) mushrooms, sliced
75 g (3 oz) Gruyère cheese

Place the potatoes in a casserole with the water, cover and microwave on **High** for 5 minutes. Drain.

Place the butter and garlic in a jug. Microwave on **High** for 30 seconds. Stir in the seasoning, nutmeg and cream. Preheat the oven on convection to 180°C.

Arrange the onions, mushrooms and potatoes in layers in a 1.2 litre (2 pint) ovenproof dish. Pour over the cream. Sprinkle with the cheese.

Place on the turntable and cook on **combination 180°C/30% microwave** for 30-35 minutes. Serve.

Microwave plus conventional
Prepare the potatoes and layer with onions and mushrooms as above. Prepare the cream and pour over the vegetables. Sprinkle with the cheese. Microwave on **Medium-High** for 13-14 minutes. Place under a preheated grill to brown.

Fan-tailed potatoes

SERVES 4-6

700 g (1½ lb) potatoes
5 tbls vegetable oil
salt

Make deep vertical slits in the potatoes about 3 mm (⅛ inch) apart.

Toss the potatoes in oil, sprinkle with salt and place on the wire rack.

Cook on **combination 250°C/30% microwave** for 35 minutes. Brush with oil 3 or 4 times during cooking.

Microwave plus conventional
Place the prepared potatoes around the edge of a large plate and microwave on **High** for 13-15 minutes, or until just tender. Re-arrange after 8 minutes. Brush with oil and place under a preheated grill to brown.

Fruity chayote

SERVES 4 as a side and 2 as a main dish

2 chayote, halved and stoned
25 g (1 oz) butter or margarine
1 small onion, finely chopped
1 tsp garam masala
50 g (2 oz) brown rice, cooked
2 tbls natural yoghurt
1 tbls fresh coriander leaves, chopped
4 kumquats, seeded and chopped
25 g (1 oz) sultanas
25 g (1 oz) no-soak apricots, chopped
150 ml (5 fl oz) orange juice
12 cashew nuts
kumquat slices, to garnish

Place the butter and onion in a 1.7 litre (3 pint) dish and microwave on **High** for 1 minute. Stir in the garam masala and microwave on **High** for 1 minute. Mix in the rice, yoghurt, coriander, kumquats, sultanas and apricots. Set aside.

Place the chayote in a shallow casserole, pour the orange juice over, cover and microwave on **High** for 10 minutes, then **combination 200°C/30% microwave** for 10 minutes. Scoop out the flesh, leaving 1 cm (½ inch) shell, chop, mix with the stuffing and pile back into the shells. Top with cashews and return to the casserole. Cook uncovered on **combination 200°C/30% microwave** for 9 minutes. Garnish and serve.

• **From top: Fan-tailed potatoes; Fruity chayote; Dauphinoise vegetables**

Queen of puddings

SERVES 6

3 egg yolks and 1 egg
50 g (2 oz) caster sugar
600 ml (1 pint) milk
3-4 drops vanilla essence
175 g (6 oz) fresh white breadcrumbs
3-4 tbls red extra fruit jam
For the topping
3 egg whites
100 g (4 oz) caster sugar

To make a custard mixture place the egg yolks, egg, sugar, milk and vanilla essence in a large jug. Whisk together. Microwave on **High** for 4 minutes, stirring twice.

Stir in the breadcrumbs and pour into a 1.2 litre (2 pint) dish. Cook on **combination 200°C/30% microwave** for 14-15 minutes, until set. Stir after 5 minutes.

Place the jam in a small bowl and microwave on **High** for 30 seconds to soften. Spread the jam over the custard, mounding it at the centre.

Whisk the egg whites until they form stiff peaks, then fold in the sugar. Pile on top of the jam leaving the centre area uncovered. Swirl into decorative peaks to represent a crown.

Cook on **combination 200°C/30% microwave** for 7 minutes.

Microwave plus conventional
Prepare the custard as above and pour over the breadcrumbs. Stir. Microwave on **High** for 5-6 minutes, stirring after 3 minutes. Top with jam and meringue as above. Microwave on **High** for 2 minutes to set the meringue. Place under a preheated grill to brown.

Fruity caramel cream

SERVES 4

4 large eggs, lightly beaten
few drops vanilla essence
25 g (1 oz) caster sugar
450 ml (3/4 pint) milk
For the caramel
75 g (3 oz) caster sugar
4 tbls water
For the filling
350 g (12 oz) mixed fresh fruit

To prepare the caramel, place the sugar and water in a 1.2 litre (2 pint) bowl and microwave on **High** for

1½ minutes. Stir to dissolve the sugar.

Continue to cook on **High** for 5-6 minutes, or until golden. Pour immediately into an 18-20 cm (7-8 inch) diameter heatproof glass ring mould.

Beat the eggs, vanilla and sugar together in a bowl. Place the milk in a large jug and microwave on **High** for 3-3½ minutes, or until nearly boiling.

Pour the milk on to the eggs and whisk together. Strain carefully over the caramel.

Stand the ring mould in a large heatproof shallow dish. Pour enough almost-boiling water into the dish to reach 5 cm (2 inches) up the outside of the mould. Cook on **combination 200°C/30% microwave** for 18-20 minutes, or until lightly set.

Leave to stand for 5 minutes. Remove the ring mould from the water and leave to cool.

Cover with a plate or foil and chill in the refrigerator for 1-2 hours. Gently loosen the edges and turn out on to a serving plate. Just before serving, fill the centre with fresh fruits.

Microwave only

Prepare the caramel and custard as above and pour into an 18-20 cm (7-8 inch) diameter heatproof glass ring mould. Place in a shallow dish containing enough almost-boiling water to reach 5 cm (2 inches) up the side of the mould. Microwave on **Medium-Low** for 15-20 minutes or until lightly set. Finish as above.

- **Left: Queen of puddings**
- **Right: Fruity caramel cream**

Apricot and almond pancakes

SERVES 4

350 g (12 oz) dried apricots, coarsely chopped
3 tbls caster sugar
2 tbls lemon juice
150 ml (5 fl oz) water
75 g (3 oz) ground almonds
2-3 drops almond essence
2 tbls flaked almonds
For the batter
100 g (4 oz) plain flour
pinch of salt
1 egg, lightly beaten
300 ml (½ pint) milk
25 g (1 oz) melted butter
vegetable oil, for frying

Make the batter first. Sift the flour and salt together. Gradually stir in the egg and half the milk. Whisk in the remaining milk and butter. Leave to stand for 30 minutes.

Heat a little oil in an 18 cm (7 inch) heavy-based frying pan. Run it around the base and sides of the pan until hot, then pour off any excess. Add sufficient batter to cover the base of the pan in a thin coat, about 1½-2 tablespoons. Turn the pan to spread the batter evenly.

Cook for 1-2 minutes until the underneath is golden brown, then toss or turn and cook the second side until golden.

Transfer the pancake to a plate. Repeat with the remaining batter to make 8 pancakes. Stack them on top of each other with greaseproof paper in between.

Either continue and make the filling or place the pancakes in a polythene bag and freeze until required.

To make the filling, place the apricots, sugar, lemon juice and water in a casserole dish. Cover with stretch film, pierce, and microwave on **High** for 6-7 minutes. Purée half the apricots in a blender or food processor.

Return the purée to the apricots in the casserole dish and stir together with the ground almonds and almond essence.

If the pancakes are frozen, defrost them on **Medium-Low** for 3-4 minutes, removing pancakes from the top and bottom as they defrost.

Spoon the filling equally over one-quarter of each pancake. Fold the pancakes over to make triangles. Place in a greased ovenproof dish and sprinkle with flaked almonds. Cook on **combination 250°C/10% microwave** for 10 minutes.

Microwave plus conventional
Place the folded pancakes, prepared as above, in a heatproof dish. Microwave on **High** for 1-1½ minutes until warm to the touch. Place under a preheated grill to brown the nuts.

Variation: Ground and chopped walnuts can be used in place of almonds.

Cherry bread and butter pudding

SERVES 4

8 slices bread, crusts removed
75 g (3 oz) butter or margarine
50 g (2 oz) glacé cherries, chopped
50 g (2 oz) sultanas
25 g (1 oz) candied peel
25 g (1 oz) currants
25 g (1 oz) chopped nuts
50 g (2 oz) caster sugar
3 eggs, lightly beaten
450 ml (¾ pint) milk

Spread the slices of bread with butter and cut each one into 4 triangles.

Place half the bread in a 1.2 litre (2 pint) ovenproof dish. Sprinkle with half the fruit, nuts and sugar. Make another layer with the remaining bread, topped with the remaining fruit, nuts and sugar.

Mix the eggs and milk together and strain over the bread. Leave to stand for 30 minutes, then cook on

• **Cherry bread and butter pudding; Apricot and almond pancakes**

combination 200°C/10% microwave for 25 minutes, or until set and golden.

Microwave plus conventional
Fill a 1.2 litre (2 pint) heatproof dish with the buttered bread, fruit and nuts as above. Mix the sugar and eggs together. Place the milk in a jug and microwave on **High** for 3½ minutes, or until almost boiling.

Mix the milk into the eggs, then strain over the bread. Microwave on **High** for 2 minutes, then cook on **Medium-Low** for 10-12 minutes, or until just set. Place under a pre-heated grill to brown.

Variation: Use a fruit bread and omit currants from the recipes.

Savarin spiral

SERVES 6

225 g (8 oz) strong plain flour
1 sachet easy-blend dried yeast
25 g (1 oz) caster sugar
4 eggs, beaten
6 tbls milk
100 g (4 oz) butter, melted
For the syrup
6 tbls clear honey
6 tbls water
3 tbls brandy
For the filling
350 g (12 oz) mixed fresh fruits

Sift the flour into a bowl and stir in the yeast and sugar. Gradually add the eggs, milk and melted butter. Beat for 3-4 minutes, then cover and leave in a warm place to rise for 20 minutes.

Beat the dough with a wooden spoon and transfer to a 20-23 cm (8-9 inch) heatproof non-metallic spiral savarin or ring mould.

Cover and leave in a warm place to rise again until double in size. This will take about 45 minutes.

Cook on **combination 250°C/30% microwave** for 15-18 minutes. Turn out on to a wire rack.

Mix the honey and water together in a bowl and microwave on **High** for 2 minutes. Stir in the brandy. Spoon over the savarin and cool.

Spoon the chopped fresh fruits into the centre and serve.

Microwave only
Prepare the savarin mixture and place in a 20-23 cm (8-9 inch) spiral non metallic ring mould. Leave in a warm place to rise and double in size. Stand on an inverted plate on the turntable and microwave on **High** for 4½-5½ minutes, or until it starts to shrink from the sides of the dish. Finish as above.

Plum lattice pie

SERVES 6

100 g (4 oz) plain flour
50 g (2 oz) wholewheat flour
pinch of salt
75 g (3 oz) butter or margarine
3 tbls cold water
450 g (1 lb) plums, stoned and quartered
1 tbls sugar crystals or caster sugar

Sift the flours together with the salt into a large mixing bowl. Rub in the fat until the mixture resembles fine breadcrumbs. Add enough water to mix to a soft dough.

Knead lightly for a few seconds. Cut off and set aside one-eighth of the pastry then roll out the remainder on a lightly floured surface. Place a 20 cm (8 inch) fluted flan ring on the turntable and line with the pastry. Prick well.

Arrange the plums in rosette fashion to fill the flan. Sprinkle with the sugar.

Roll out the remaining pastry and cut it into 5 mm (¼ inch) strips. Twist them and arrange over the fruit in a lattice pattern.

Cook on **combination 230°C/10% microwave** for 15 minutes.

Microwave only
Line a non-metallic fluted flan ring with the pastry and prick it well. Line the base with a sheet of absorbent paper and microwave on **High** for 4 minutes, removing the paper after 3 minutes. Place the strips of pastry in a lattice pattern on a sheet of greaseproof paper. Microwave on **High** for 1½-2 minutes.

Place the plums in a shallow dish, sprinkle with sugar and cover with stretch film. Pierce the film and microwave on **High** for 4 minutes, or until the fruit is just tender. Rearrange the fruit after 2 minutes. Carefully arrange the fruit in the pastry base. Top with the lattice and serve.

If wished you can make in advance and reheat for 30 seconds on **High** before serving.

Variation: Use all wholewheat flour for the pastry. The fruit can be varied according to the season. In the summer use apricots or gooseberries. If using soft fruits such as raspberries cook the fruit for slightly less time.

- **Left: Savarin spiral**
- **Right: Plum lattice pie**

Strawberry shortcakes

SERVES 4

100 g (4 oz) butter
50 g (2 oz) caster sugar
50 g (2 oz) plain flour
50 g (2 oz) rice flour
50 g (2 oz) wholemeal flour
For the filling
142 ml (5 fl oz) carton whipping cream, whipped
175-225 g (6-8 oz) strawberries

Cream the butter until soft. Add the sugar and beat until pale and fluffy.

Fold in the flours and knead until the mixture binds together to form a dough.

Roll the dough out on a lightly floured surface to a thickness of 5 mm (¼ inch). Cut out 8 rounds 9 cm (3½ inches) in diameter, using a fluted cutter.

Divide the rounds between two sheets of silicone paper. Place one on the turntable and the other on the wire rack. Cook on **combination 220°C/10% microwave** for 6 minutes. Change shelf positions and cook for a further 6 minutes.

Cut 4 of the rounds into quarters. Leave the shortcake to cool on a wire rack.

Pile whipped cream and strawberries on top of the whole rounds and decorate with shortcake quarters.

Microwave only
Prepare, roll out and cut the dough into 8 rounds as above. Cook in 2 batches on the turntable only. Microwave each batch on **High** for 3 minutes. Finish as above.

- **Left: Strawberry shortcakes**
- **Right: Apple and hazelnut galette**

Apple and hazelnut galette

SERVES 6-8

75 g (3 oz) hazelnuts
75 g (3 oz) butter or margarine
25 g (1 oz) caster sugar
120 g (4½ oz) plain flour
For the filling
450 g (1 lb) green apples, peeled, cored and sliced
rind and juice 1 lemon
1 tbls caster sugar
25 g (1 oz) sultanas
25 g (1 oz) orange peel, finely chopped
½ tsp ground cinnamon
3 tbls whipping cream, whipped, to decorate

Place the hazelnuts on a plate and microwave on **High** for 4-5 minutes to brown. Stir 2 or 3 times. Reserve 8 nuts and grind the remainder in a food processor or blender.

Beat the butter and sugar together until light and fluffy. Stir in the flour and hazelnuts and mix to a ball, kneading well. Chill for 30 minutes.

Divide the mixture into two and roll each into a 20 cm (8 inch) round. Prick well and place one on the turntable and the other on the wire rack lined with greaseproof paper. Cook on **combination 200°C/ 10% microwave** for 6 minutes. Change shelf positions and cook for a further 6-9 minutes.

Remove the rounds and mark one of them into 8. Leave until cold.

To prepare the filling, place the apples, lemon rind and juice, and caster sugar in a casserole dish and microwave on **High** for 4 minutes. Add the sultanas, orange peel and cinnamon and microwave on **High** for 2 minutes. Stir and leave to cool.

Cut the marked round into 8 triangles. Cover the whole round with the filling and place the cut portions on top. Pipe a cream rosette on each portion and decorate each with a whole hazelnut.

Microwave only
Prepare the biscuit rounds as above. Place each round on a sheet of greaseproof paper and microwave one by one on **High** for 2¾-3¼ minutes.

Finish as above.

• Raspberry and kiwi mille-feuille

Raspberry and kiwi mille-feuille

MAKES 5-6 SLICES

225 g (8 oz) puff pastry
142 ml (5 fl oz) carton whipping cream, whipped
4 tbls greengage or kiwi fruit jam
175 g (6 oz) raspberries
2 kiwi fruit, peeled and sliced

Preheat the oven on convection to 250°C. On a lightly floured surface, roll out the pastry to a rectangle measuring 23 × 30 cm (9 × 12 inches). Cut into 3 strips of 23 × 10 cm (9 × 4 inches).

Prick the strips all over with a fork and place 2 on the lightly greased turntable. Place the third on the wire rack lined with greaseproof paper.

Cook on **combination 250°C/30% microwave** for 10 minutes. Remove the strips after 4 minutes and let the steam out of the pastry by pressing it lightly with a fork.

While they are warm, trim the strips to equal sizes with straight edges. Leave on a cooling rack until cold.

Divide the cream into 3, spread 2 pieces of pastry first with jam, then a layer of cream. Top one with raspberries, reserving a few of the best to decorate the top, and the other with kiwi fruit. Place the kiwi layer on top of the raspberries. Top with the remaining pastry layer. Decorate with the remaining cream and fruit. Brush with jam to gloss. If the jam is too thick, microwave for a few seconds to soften. Serve sliced.

Microwave only:
Roll out the pastry to a rectangle 23 × 10 cm (9 × 4 inches). Place on a double thickness of absorbent paper on the turntable. Cover with another piece of absorbent paper. Microwave on **High** for 4-5 minutes, until well risen and firm. Remove paper and place pastry on a rack to cool, then cut horizontally into three. Assemble as above.

Wholemeal bread rolls

MAKES 12

225 g (8 oz) strong plain flour
225 g (8 oz) strong plain wholewheat flour
1 sachet easy-blend dried yeast
1 tsp salt
300 ml (½ pint) lukewarm milk
1 egg, lightly beaten
beaten egg, to glaze
wheatgerm, sesame seeds or poppy seeds to sprinkle

Mix the flours together with the yeast and salt. Add the milk and egg and knead together for 5-10 minutes.

Return the dough to a lightly greased bowl. Cover and leave in a warm place until it has doubled in size.

To speed the rising process, microwave on **High** for 15 secconds. Leave to stand for 10 minutes. Repeat twice more. Leave, covered until doubled in size.

Knead the dough lightly on a floured surface. Divide into 12 and shape into rolls. Place on the turntable and brush the rolls with beaten egg. Sprinkle with wheatgerm, sesame seeds or poppy seeds and leave for 10 minutes.

Meanwhile preheat the oven on convection to 220°C. Cook on **combination 220°C/30% microwave** for 12 minutes. Transfer to a cooling rack and leave to cool.

• **Wholemeal bread rolls**

Herby cheese loaf ring

SERVES 6-8

350 g (12 oz) strong plain flour
100 g (4 oz) plain wholemeal flour
1 tsp salt
½ tsp mustard powder
1 sachet easy-blend yeast
1 tbls mixed fresh herbs, chopped
2 tbls fresh parsley, chopped
100 g (4 oz) mature Cheddar cheese, grated
50 g (2 oz) butter, melted
75 ml (3 fl oz) lukewarm milk
150 ml (5 fl oz) lukewarm water
beaten egg, to glaze

Place the flours, salt, mustard, yeast, herbs and all but 1 tbls of the cheese in a large bowl and mix together.

Add the butter, milk and water and mix to a soft dough. Knead for 5-10 minutes, until smooth.

Return the dough to a lightly greased bowl. Cover and leave in a warm place until it has doubled in size.

To speed the rising process, microwave on **High** for 15 seconds. Leave to stand for 10 minutes. Repeat twice more. Leave, covered, until double in size.

Form the dough into a round flat loaf. Make a hole in the centre. Rotate a wooden spoon in the hole to make it larger, forming a ring. Make shallow cuts in the top of the loaf. Brush with beaten egg and sprinkle with the remaining cheese.

Place on the turntable and leave for 10 minutes to rise. Meanwhile, preheat the oven on convection to 220°C. Cook on **combination 220°C/10% microwave** for 15 minutes.

- **Top: Cheese palmiers**
- **Bottom: Herby cheese loaf ring**

Cheese palmiers

MAKES 9

150 g (6 oz) puff pastry, defrosted if frozen
3 tbls Parmesan cheese, grated
beaten egg, to glaze
For the filling
100 g (4 oz) full fat soft cheese
3 tbls milk
¼ tsp paprika
pinch of celery salt
For decoration
red and black lumpfish roe
stuffed olives, sliced
walnut halves
smoked salmon strips

Roll out the pastry into an oblong 30 × 10 cm (12 × 4 inches). Sprinkle with 1 tbls cheese. Fold the top third of the pastry down over the centre, and the bottom third up over it. Seal the edges, give the pastry a half turn, roll out and repeat the process with another tablespoon of cheese.

Roll and fold the pastry once more. Wrap and chill for 30 minutes.

Roll out into a rectangle 25 × 20 cm (10 × 8 inches). Trim the edges neatly and brush the whole surface with egg. Fold the long sides to the centre. Brush with egg. Bring the folded edges to the centre to make a long strip about 6 cm (2½ inches) wide. Press the strip together and trim the ends. Cut into eighteen 1 cm (½ inch) slices.

Place the slices, spaced apart, on a sheet of greaseproof paper and place on the turntable. Sprinkle the remaining cheese over the tops. Cook on **combination 250°C/30% microwave** for 14-16 minutes. Leave to cool on a wire rack.

To make the filling, mix together the cheese, milk and paprika. Season with celery salt. Sandwich the palmiers together with half the cheese mixture. Pipe the remaining filling on the top and decorate with roe, olive slices, walnuts and smoked salmon.

Nutty fruit cake

MAKES 8-10 SLICES

175 g (6 oz) butter or margarine
175 g (6 oz) light brown soft sugar
3 eggs
225 g (8 oz) plain flour
½ tsp baking powder
2 tsp ground mixed spice
¼ tsp ground cinnamon
¼ tsp ground nutmeg
pinch of salt
150 g (5 oz) currants
75 g (3 oz) raisins
75 g (3 oz) sultanas
25 g (1 oz) mixed peel, chopped
25 g (1 oz) glacé cherries, chopped
50 g (2 oz) almonds, chopped
2-3 tbls milk
For the decoration
split almonds
walnut halves
hazelnuts

Line an 18 cm (7 inch) round cake tin with greased greaseproof paper.

Cream the butter or margarine and sugar together until pale and fluffy. Gradually beat in the eggs. Mix the flour, baking powder, spices, salt, fruit and chopped almonds together and fold in. Stir in the milk, to give a dropping consistency.

Turn the mixture into the prepared tin and make a slight hollow in the centre. Place on the rack and cook on **combination 160°C/10% microwave** for 10 minutes. Remove from the oven and arrange rings of nuts on top to decorate. Cook on **combination 160°C/10% microwave** for a further 20-25 minutes. When the cake is cooked a skewer inserted in the centre should come out clean.

Leave the cake to cool slightly before turning it out of the tin. Stand it on a wire rack to cool.

Microwave only
Prepare the cake mixture and place in a 20 cm (8 inch) microwave-safe dish. Place on an upturned plate in the microwave oven and cook on **Medium-Low** for 15 minutes. Top with nuts and cook for a further 15-20 minutes. It will still be moist in the centre of the top, but will be cooked through by the time it has cooled down.

Strawberry sponge turnovers

MAKES 6

3 egg yolks
40 g (1½ oz) caster sugar
25 g (1 oz) plain flour
1 tbls cornflour
pinch of salt
15 g (½ oz) butter, melted
2 egg whites
icing sugar, for dusting
For the filling
142 ml (5 fl oz) carton whipping cream, whipped
100 g (4 oz) fresh strawberries, hulled and halved

- **Left: Strawberry sponge turnovers**
- **Right: Nutty fruit cake**

Draw 3 circles 13 cm (5 inches) in diameter on each of two sheets of silicone paper the size of the turntable. Place one on the turntable and the other on a baking sheet on top of the wire rack.

Preheat the oven on convection to 200°C.

Whisk the egg yolks with half the sugar in a bowl, until thick and creamy.

Sift the flours together with the salt. Fold into the egg yolk mixture with the melted butter.

Whisk the egg whites until they form stiff peaks. Fold in the remaining sugar. Fold in to the flour and egg mixture.

Pipe or spoon on to the circles and spread gently to cover. Cook on **combination 200°C/10% microwave** for 5-6 minutes, or until golden brown and springy when lightly touched.

Place the sponge rounds upside down on a clean teatowel and fold them in half carefully. Leave to cool under the teatowel. Fill with the cream and fruit, sprinkle with icing sugar and serve.

Microwave only
Prepare the sponges as above and cook in 2 batches of three. Microwave each batch on **High** for 1½-1¾ minutes. Finish as above.

Variation: Use fresh raspberries, redcurrants or seedless grapes in place of the strawberries.

Orange nut croissants

MAKES 12

225 g (8 oz) strong plain flour
1 sachet easy-blend yeast
pinch of salt
100 g (4 oz) butter
120 ml (4 fl oz) lukewarm milk
1 egg, lightly beaten
1 egg yolk, beaten, to glaze
For the filling
75 g (3 oz) ground almonds
grated rind and juice 1 orange
1 tbls orange liqueur
1 tbls candied orange peel
25 g (1 oz) caster sugar

Sift the flour and mix in the yeast and salt. Place 50 g (2 oz) butter in a small bowl and microwave on **High** for 45-60 seconds, to melt. Stir into the flour with the milk and whole egg. Knead to a smooth dough.

Cover and leave to rise for 30 minutes. Roll out on a lightly floured surface into an oblong about 2.5 cm (½ inch) thick. Dot half the remaining butter over the top two-thirds. Fold the bottom third up over the centre and the top section down over that. Press the edges together firmly. Turn a quarter.

Roll out again into an oblong and fold as above. Chill for 15 minutes. Repeat the two-rolling process with the remaining butter. Chill again for 30 minutes.

Mix the filling together well. Place in the centre of each triangle. Roll up lengthways and curve.

Place the croissants on two sheets of greased greaseproof paper and place on the wire rack and turntable. Leave to rise for 15-20 minutes.

Preheat the oven on convection to 230°C.

Brush the croissants with beaten egg yolk and cook on **combination 230°C/10% microwave** for 10 minutes. Change the shelf positions after 4 minutes.

Choc-orange Viennese whirls

MAKES 6

100 g (4 oz) butter
25 g (1 oz) icing sugar, sifted
150 g (5 oz) plain flour
finely grated rind 1 orange
50 g (2 oz) orange-flavoured milk chocolate, broken into pieces
142 ml (5 fl oz) carton whipping cream, whipped
grated orange rind, to decorate

Place the butter in a mixing bowl and beat until soft. Add the icing sugar, flour and orange rind and beat together. Add 1-2 tsp milk if the mixture seems a little stiff.

Place in a piping bag fitted with a large star nozzle. Pipe 12 rosettes on to the lightly greased turntable.

Cook on **combination 200°C/10% microwave** for 12 minutes, or until just beginning to turn golden brown. Remove to a wire rack and leave to cool.

Place the chocolate in a bowl and microwave on **Medium** for 1-1½ minutes, stirring twice. Place in a small greaseproof piping bag, cut a small piece off the end to make a hole and drizzle the chocolate over the cold biscuits. Leave to set.

Sandwich together with whipped cream, sprinkle with grated orange rind and serve.

Note
These biscuits are best cooked in a conventional oven, if a combination oven is not available.

Prune or apricot spiced scones

MAKES 12

225 g (8 oz) self-raising flour
½ tsp salt
1 tsp baking powder
50 g (2 oz) butter or margarine
1 tbls caster sugar
50 g (2 oz) no-soak prunes or dried apricots, chopped
1 tsp ground mixed spice
150 ml (¼ pint) milk
beaten egg or milk, to glaze
To serve
butter curls or whipped cream
3-4 tbls jam or honey

Preheat the oven to 220°C. Sift the flour, salt and baking powder together. Rub in the butter or margarine until the mixture resembles fine breadcrumbs. Stir in the sugar, fruit and mixed spice.

Stir in sufficient milk to give a fairly soft dough. Knead lightly on a floured surface, then roll out lightly to about 2 cm (¾ inch) thick.

Cut the dough into rounds with a 5 cm (2 inch) fluted pastry cutter. Place on a large plate or baking sheet on the wire rack. Brush with egg or milk to glaze and cook on **combination 230°C/10% microwave** for 9-10 minutes. Serve with butter curls and honey or whipped cream and jam.

Microwave plus conventional
Prepare the dough and cut into rounds as above. Cook in two batches, placed around the edge of the turntable. Microwave on **High** for 1¾-2¼ minutes. If wished, place under a preheated grill to brown.

Variation: Cut into triangles with a sharp knife and cook as above.

• **Prune spiced scones; Orange nut croissants; Choc-orange Viennese whirls**

INDEX